Quiet Places, Morning Walks

Notes Between Secular and Sacred

Poems by

Gene G. Bradbury

BookWilde Children's Books Plus

Quiet Places, Morning Walks
Poems by Gene G. Bradbury
Copyright ©2014 by Gene G. Bradbury

ISBN 978-0-9897585-4-3

Printed in the United States
by Createspace Independent Publishing Platform

Book design/prepress: Kate Weisel, weiselcreative.com

All inquiries should be addressed to
BookWilde Children's Books Plus
422 Williamson Rd.
Sequim, WA 98382
www.genegbradbury.com

Dedication

To my friends at Dungeness Valley Lutheran Church in Sequim for their commitment to serving others and ministering to all who enter their doors.

And to my friends at Trinity Lutheran Church in Port Angeles, always welcoming and faithful in their mission.

We should think sacredly, with devotion.
This is one thing we can do magnanimously.

> Henry David Thoreau: Journals
> July 27, Tuesday 4 P.M., 1852

Preface

The title **Quiet Places, Morning Walks** indicates my preference for quiet time. These poems, reflections, and Psalm Notes can be used any time during the day. A quiet moment with a cup of coffee and a book is my personal preference for solitude.

I hope you will find your own special time whether morning, noon, or evening to use this book and enter a quiet place. In a busy and sometimes invasive world, we often neglect this special gift. Time alone with our thoughts in a spirit of stillness is an invitation to enrich our day.

About the contents of this small book:

Morning Litanies offer a simple thought, in haiku form to begin the day.

Morning Walks are short essays that introduce four themes: solitude, wakefulness, loneliness, and celebration. Each begins a new section of poetry.

Psalm Notes introduce each poem in the collection. It is a personal response to a selected verse, like the applause at a concert after the music is played. I have also rendered the Psalm Notes in haiku form, three lines of five syllables, seven syllables, five syllables.

Evening Songs are simple thoughts at the end of day that welcome peaceful rest.

The subtitle: *Notes Between Secular and Sacred* indicates the two worlds in which we walk. While we are all in some sense spiritual people, we live in the physical world. These meditations are an attempt to find the meeting ground between the two worlds in the hope that they might speak to the reality of the one and our need for the other.

Any of these themes may be used in the sequence the reader finds most helpful. Above all, you are invited to enjoy *Quiet Places, Morning Walks.*

The Author

Contents

Morning Litanies in Haiku

Monday:
>Wake me this morning,
>alive to what this day brings
>Open eyes and ears.

Tuesday:
>In divine moments,
>begin the day in silence,
>folded in quiet.

Wednesday:
>My cup before me
>tasting and smelling of life.
>Fill it with delight.

Thursday:
>What have I to give:
>a kind word of thanks to share
>love instead of hate.

Friday:
>Give me this fifth day
>body peace and mind at rest
>gentleness to live.

Saturday:
>Moments come at times
>to sit, reflect, and receive
>divine tenderness.

Sunday:
>Look to morning light,
>having rested through the night
>alive to the day.

Morning Walks:
SOLITUDE

On my desk is a photograph of a log cabin. The ground is white and snow clings to tall pines. The photograph was a gift from my wife who bears with my dream of living in the woods.

I seek a place where I might withdraw into the silent companionship of books and quiet surroundings; to breathe outside the tangle of tasks and obligations.
"Come, be still." But am I afraid of being alone?

Silence can be uncomfortable, and yet it is essential to our well-being. Henry Nouwen suggests one of the benefits of solitude is that we take the other with us. When this happens, our relationship deepens. When we are alone, space is cleared to think of other people in our lives.

A quiet place calls us to examine ourselves, our wants, our desires, and our needs. If the day's calendar fills completely we experience fatigue, depression, and anger. If we are depressed we have no time for ourselves. If we are angry, we blame others for requiring too much of our time.

Who is responsible for setting aside time for us to listen to our interior pulse?

Where, where can I go?
If I fly with morning wings
you are there for me.
　　Psalm Note: 139:7

Where Spirits Speak

Down there,
down deep,
Down, down,
where spirits speak.

Stay still,
small toad
among today's traffic,
clouds of pavement dust.

Wait for silence,
wheels to pass by,
distractions fall away,
leap now in perfect time,

a kairos moment
when streets are clear,
the heart is stilled,
you are there.

Give ear to my words,
hear the sounds of my crying
this morning I pray.
  Psalm Note: 5:1-3

Early Morning

Before the light
or hint of light,
before morning song,
before a child's fitful cry,
in the twilight dawn
when nothing stirs but me,
I give myself to quiet
and rest myself in Thee.

Righteousness and peace will kiss,
love and faithfulness will meet,
and all will be well.
  Psalm Note: 85:10-12

From the Still Night

From the still night
begins the day,
following a quiet path,
pointing,
whispering:

Walk in peace.
  Walk in silence.
    Walk in stillness.

From the still day
begins the night,
recalling quiet paths,
pointing,
whispering:

Sleep in peace
  Sleep in silence
    Sleep in stillness.

The pastures overflow,
the hills rejoice everywhere,
meadows clothe themselves.
    Psalm Note: 65:12, 13

Gathering Elders

On green pasture hills,
nod yellowed daises,
spruce elders listen
in ruffled dark gowns,
point needle sharp fingers
at cumulus skies,
wave anxious branches
as wind passes by.

Hear and be gracious.
Turn my mourning to dancing,
clothe me with gladness.
   Psalm Note: 30:10, 11

Empathic Listener

Listen to river-rain,
silently waiting,
    flowing-pain,
    one who...
stands at the river's edge.

Feel a moment's indecision,
    interior spray,
    water's dark passing,
    silently flow, divine prayer,
standing, listening, waiting.

Stay in the moment,
    let shadows pass,
    feel wet grace
    in silence, hearing,
build a bridge, a place to walk.

Give me a clean heart,
a right spirit within me
leave me not alone.
   Psalm Note: 51:10,12

Flow Me a River

Flow me a river
past stale dank towns
with telltale clocks
committee laid tables.

Flow me a river
where leaves pale
in cold autumn breeze,
to fall on pewter water.

Give swift river glide,
by crippled paths
where limping soldiers
once marched to war.

Let freshet spray
splash my bough
sing verses and song
of halcyon days.

You have searched me
You know my thoughts from afar
You know me deeply.
   Psalm Note: 139:1,2

The Place of Soul

Enter the place of soul,
circumnavigate the self,
go where the heart beats
rhythmically like oars over
water, pulling one to center,
past Dante's warning gates,
"Beware all who enter here."
Spiral down subconscious steps,
follow footprints of those who
passed this way before,
and find what it is like
to be known from afar,
to be known deeply.

Morning Walks: WAKEFULNESS

Time alone invites us to listen to the interior self. With distractions turned off and noise reduced, we are prepared to receive. I am haunted by the words of Henry David Thoreau:

> "I listen from time to time to hear the hounds of silence baying the moon, . . .the silence sings. It is musical. I remember a night when it was audible. I hear the unspeakable."

To hear the unspeakable can also be frightening. From inside a forest cabin the sounds of the night invite the outside in. Hearing becomes sharper. Being alone trains our ears to pay attention.

Our ability to see also increases when we are alone. We pay more attention to our surroundings. When we are always on the way someplace we reduce our ability to see. We can become blind to things around us and miss the surprises along the way.

A quiet place calls us to be watchful, to listen and see. Walk a forest path or a sandy beach. The sound of one's own footsteps and the beat of one's own heart are sometimes company enough.

I will sing to God
who deals bountifully with me,
and so I will sing.
    Psalm Note: 13:6

There Are Miracles in the Morning

When sun kisses Iowa cornstalks,
red-winged blackbirds tilt their heads
on fence posts to catch a glint of light.

In Kansas, morning leans fresh
over winter wheat, swelling it like waves,
sunlight dresses the pheasant's wing.

When Montana's first light passes
along the Blackfoot River, fly-fishermen
cast lines before kingfisher's eye.

In Washington the eastern sun climbs
Mt. Olympus to paint snow bright,
as a blue heron waits stick still.

There are miracles in the morning.

Before the holy
be still and wait patiently
rest and do not fret.
Psalm Note: 37:7

The Room Beyond

A changing light in
grey and timeless sky
moves shadows
across Heron Pond.

He arrives as herons do,
a melancholy prophet
to stand on glass
unmoving, waiting.

A silent bird,
a wordless morning,
a feathered charm
on a silver bracelet.

I gaze silently through
a six-paned window
while Vermeer paints
the room beyond.

I will sing at dawn.
I will make a melody.
Wake my soul and sing.
    Psalm Note: 108:1

I Am Finch

From highest stem,
invisible against sunlight,
finch sings her melody:
"I am finch, I am me,
it's my world atop this tree."

We, earthbound, fumble below
try to discover who we are,
not content just to be,
struggle here without a song
tired, uncertain, and alone.

But, not this morning, for
a small speck against the sky
sings, delighted just to be,
a finch on the Diadora tree
invites me to be me.

Let words from my mouth
and the thoughts of my own heart
be found worthy now.
    Psalm Note: 19:14

A Word

A worthy word,
conceive in me,
formed in silence,

letters with body,
vowels with limbs,
moved to birth,

born of spirit,
ready the womb,
grant me speech.

O Spirit-sent words
melting words that make winds blow
and the waters flow.
    Psalm Note: 147: 18

Lady of the Lake

Voices soar over water,
sailing low like Noah's dove,
flap winged-words…
whispering, whispering.

In misty river silence
unfold my fledgling thoughts,
preen them for right moments
to fly wistfully free.

Let not my words
too soon spoken
return, tired like raven
finding no land.

You have made the moon
and the sun's time for setting
marking the seasons.
  Psalm Note: 104:19

All I Remember Is . . .

All I remember is . . .
wind over lake water,
sunlight's path,
where dragonflies played,
and longing to walk
on water like Jesus.

There rose
a quiet still breath,
sun's warm rayed arms
inviting me,
come, step, risk,
believe you can.

All I remember is . . .
sunlight setting,
wind ceasing,
shadows folding,
water painted a color,
of flamingo wings.

Yes, this is the day
to enjoy all that is made.
Rejoice and be glad.
  Psalm Note: 118:24

Grace of Day

When spoke
the aspen tree
by westerly wind,
I raised my eyes
to falling leaves;
  it was then,
  it was then,
I saw light
filtered sky
skate shadows
upon the ground;
  It was then,
  It was then,
night crept away.
I showered under
Aspen leaves
in the grace of day.

Boundaries are fixed
all the seasons of the earth
summer and winter.
  Psalm Note: 74:17

Eyes of the River

River flow to
Juan de Fuca,
sun-glint eyes,
foaming dark water,

spring current swift,
gamboling horsemen,
or staggering derelict,
winter's tramp.

Pass swiftly along
gather wet visions
fishermen, heron,
Canadian fowl,

flow river flow
freshet or ramble
meandering youth
toward Puget Sound.

Be still, yes, be still
know the spirit lives in us
breathe stillness and know.
     Psalm Note: 46:10

The Way It Was

Take away
the distant tractor,
a roofer downhill,
voices from the river
school-yard bell,
my presence
voice, song, breath.
What is left:
prairie quiet,
finch song,
everything still
except the bee.

Look at the heavens
moon and stars established
be mindful of them.
   Psalm Note: 8:3,4

Dreams

I wake
to moon-falling light
soft upon my pillow.

Stars from afar
slide lightly down
the sheen of the moon.

Snow falls quietly
from heaven's great store.
Dare I ask for anything more.

Forget not the poor
raise up the poor and lowly
that they may give thanks.
    Psalm Note: 74:21

Tears Like Rain

I will stand in rain
under dark clouds,
gather the tears
of those far away;
feel their wet-weeping
run down my face,
for who can deny
that we, like they,
live under like sky.

When in suffering
my own tears are shed,
I'll look to the clouds
passing high overhead,
let my weeping
be carried aloft to
drop as rain
on those far off,
who share like pain.

Morning Walks:
LONELINESS

Solitude and loneliness are not the same thing. Loneliness can sometimes seem sad; but it need be neither good nor bad.
It can be a time of greater intensity when we look deeper into ourselves. Being alone in our thoughts can bring us closer to others.

Solitude and loneliness are two dimensions of ourselves.
Solitude opens us to the wider world. Time by ourselves enables us to experience our own loneliness and to better understand the loneliness that pervades our world.

In times of loneliness I find myself turning the pages of a book and remembering the words of an anonymous writer:
"We read to know that we are not alone." How true that is.
An author may write about my experience. Reading enriches us. But it doesn't stop there. Reading widens our experience and knowledge of others.

I go to a place of solitude to be alone and restore myself.
This may be in the company of those writers who are quietly present in their books. This kind of solitude gives me something to take back into the community where I live.

Marvel at thy works,
wonderful are they to tell,
the miracles done.
    Psalm Note: 105:5

The Irises

> The irises have wilted
> on lily pond
> by the bridge.
>
> I remember them
> as they were in spring,
> now that they are gone.

O send out your light.
Let your light and truth lead me
to your dwelling place.
  Psalm Note: 43:3

Behold the Stars

Where asphalt ends
  grass begins,
    winter spruce whispers,
    "Look up, see the stars,
    beholding you."

When all seems dark
  stars are not lost.
  Look deeply,
  sorrow burns up
  in bright light.

Distant stars
  invite you,
    sit at their hearth fire,
    be warmed in their light,
    find comfort tonight.

Now deep calls to deep
and the cataracts thunder
as waves roll over me.
  Psalm Note: 42:7

Beverly Beach

Rip-rabble waves,
Kelp carpet, mussel-shell,
bleached dishevelment debris,
sandy prints, lost tennis shoe,
tangled filament fishing line,
and always,
the incoming smile of the sea.

Teach me the right way
with an undivided heart.
Let me walk in truth.
    Psalm Note: 86:11

Free Fall

Thoughts fall to earth
leaves from the maple,
scattering beauty across
our cerebral landscape
where we attempt

to rake them into neat piles,
acceptable, predictable, until
a rogue wind catches them,
swirls them in air,
lifts them to sky, and

we stand alone, rake in hand.

The storm is made still,
waves of the sea are hushed,
and there is quiet.
    Psalm Note: 107: 29, 30

Each Day

> If you have nothing to say,
> let the day write itself,
> wait, be still, listen.
>
> It is enough for
> hymns to sing their song,
> for rivers to find their way,
> for birds to have voices.
>
> Let clouds pass silently,
> to gather moisture
> for tomorrow.

With you my good friend,
my familiar companion,
I share pleasant times.
Psalm Note: 55:13, 14

My Visit

I left your tea cup
near the sofa,
a note on the buffet,
my poem upon your table,
for you to read
at close of day.

I returned your book,
read in sunshine
quietly on the porch,
and have taken with me
kindness spoken,
our friendship renewed.

Should I find darkness,
and light around me grow dark,
in me light will shine.
   Psalm Note: 139:11,12

Light on Snow

Where did I go in the night
below the conscious seam;
to a church where choirs sing,
a restaurant I did not know
with friends from long ago.
From places of restless sleep
I awake above the dream
to light on snow

I will both lie down,
lie down and sleep peacefully,
in safety I'll lie.
    Psalm Note: 4:8

Winter Song

Speak not to me of springtime
with snow upon the hills.
Don't speak to me of lilacs
when skies grow dark and gray.

Speak to me of hearth fire,
an afghan upon my lap,
a book open before me,
an intermittent nap.

The day pours forth speech,
the night declares knowledge, yet,
their voice is not heard.
    Psalm Note: 19:2

Reading

Reading
ruffles my spirit
like birds
eager to fly, words
twist, turn, and bring
tears to my eye;

or perch lightly
upon moving lips,
to erupt in spirits,
of eager laughter,
and free-fall into
the arms of books.

Morning Walks: CELEBRATIONS

Celebrations are milestones we pass along the way. Our lives are measured by birthdays and special moments with our families at Thanksgiving and Christmas. Celebrations help us remember and relive times and places: "Remember when."

More importantly, celebrations connect us closely with each other on those occasions of births, marriages, and times of death.

Our celebrations mark us with laughter and crying. They create lasting memories that we review through photographs and stories. Celebrations lift our lives to new levels and our relationships to new heights.

Some of our celebrations grow from the soil of our spiritual lives. We recall baptisms, bar mitzvahs, children's Christmas programs where everything goes wrong. We share them again and again in quiet moments together.

In my secret heart
oh teach me truth and wisdom.
This is my desire.
  Psalm Note: 51:6

The Quiet of Snow
Hannah's birthday, 2010

I am writing poetry today
and you are twenty-six.
I wonder if
the light falling snow
can speak for me, and say. . .

May the lightness of white stars
fall upon your days, and bring
beauty to your life, not
in heavy blizzard or blinding light,
but quiet upon your face.

It will say, stretch out your arms,
open your hands to the sky,
catch each gentle flake
fresh upon your eyes
and know how precious life is.

The Spirit goes forth
and renews the face of earth
creating all things.
  Psalm Note: 104:30

They Waited
(Pentecost)

Friends
covered in darkness
of thick-knowing loss.
Nerves weave
a silk web over the room
binding them in grief.

It was the first waiting.

A voice clipped their net,
"Peace be with you."
He lifted tomb-bleared eyes,
"Be not afraid, it is I."
Thomas missed it,
would not believe.

It was the second waiting.

"Go to Galilee!"
They huddled again, when . . .
wisp of air touched the fiber,
tightened, snapped,
fire tongued their faces,
knit them together, one breath.

It was the third waiting.

The Lord is my rock,
the sure place I take refuge,
my fortress, my strength.
     Psalm Note: 18:2

Baptized

A rock shaped by water,
carved below waterfalls.
Remember
wetness spilled from above,
softened by word,
cleansed by promise,
set free to be a river.

Pearlescence

The Spirit is near,
near to all those who call out,
and truly seek truth.
  Psalm Note: 145:18

The prayer class gathered
in a circle of uplifted faces,
like a pearl necklace,
strung by invisible thread.

Each of us, a speck of
Abraham's promised sand,
birthed from a single grain,
now a circle of bright thought.

It snowed in the city,
round crystal flakes,
landing on still tongues,
lifted to the heavens.

Quiet, brilliant, numberless
white stars, floating down
frozen pearls from above,
silent messengers,

while we listened indoors
linked by words, waiting for
prayer to fall quiet as snow,
until the thread broke,

spilling pearls from chairs,
bounced across the floor,
out the classroom door,
into the parking lot; and

we looked into a snowy sky
this pearl rosary, mouths open
to receive divine grace,
pearlesence, eternal shine.

Let seas roar and foam,
floods clap their hands together,
the hills sing for joy.
　　Psalm Note: 98:7

Her Birthday

He springs from her,
black lab of ocean spray.
Barefoot she smiles,
"It's beautiful," she says.
"Yes, it is," I reply.
On wet sand she's away,
shoes in hand, turns,
"It's my birthday!"
Alone on her birthday,
but no...
a frolicking companion
splashes, her celebration.

Show me life's pathway.
In your presence there is joy,
there I will find life.
    Psalm Note: 16:11b

Night Rain

Around my bed
in me
through me
over me
baptism's gift.

Not Noah's rain,
Abraham's rain,
promise wet,
over the ground,
to refresh the dead.

At-one-ment:
it, we, them,
tears of rain
into the earth
and out again.

We wither away,
life like an evening shadow,
disappears on grass.
    Psalm Note: 102:11

One Winter Day

One winter day
I will be an old man,
a face in the window
peering out on falling snow.

I will stare at the magnolia tree
and ponder through cold panes
how it feels to be stripped bare
icy snow upon my limbs.

And I will say to the tree,
I know who you are
peering back at me
through cold glass, growing old.

Your lovingkindness
I see now before my eyes.
Let me walk in truth.
    Psalm Note: 26:3

Benches

Here's a bench, sit a spell
we'll compose questions
asked before, and agree,
"Yes, that's how it is."

We'll walk on
stumble now and then
along gravel paths
to another bench, and say,
"What's our talk of today?"

Years will pass,
our pace slower now
bench to bench,
speak without words,
sit silently, nodding, "yes."

One day, arthritis pains,
canes of no consequence,
we'll remember benches
where we sat, together
friends in confidence.

Hear my cry, O God.
Know when my heart becomes faint,
show me a safe place.
  Psalm Note: 61:2

At the Stile

> I come to a stile,
> end of a familiar path,
> an exit-entrance gate,
> and raise a rusted latch.
> One longing glance back
> to fields of flower-bloom:
> my eyes follow footprints
> to this place, where now
> I ask: Should I go through
> to new meadows of grass
> I do not know and meander
> uncertain valleys below?

Evening Songs in Haiku

Monday:
>As I spent the day
>in gifts of incoming tide,
>thanks for ebbing light.

Tuesday:
>I walked the bridge
>between morning and evening
>and came to day's end.

Wednesday:
>I woke to bird song,
>finches are quiet tonight,
>morning and evening.

Thursday:
>Look back on today
>how my footprints wandered.
>Tonight they find rest.

Friday:
>This week now filled
>gifts unwrapped, clear the space
>sit still, breath at last.

Saturday:
>Enter night's quiet,
>pull the shade, draw the curtains
>silence end of day.

Sunday:
>Bestow night's soft grace,
>enfolding breath, Sabbath rest.
>Hear owl passing by.

Poems previously published

Early Morning	*Traveling in Company,* 2013
From the Still Night	*Traveling in Company,* 2013
Empathic Listener	*Traveling in Company,* 2013
I Am Finch	*An Anthology of Northwest Poets,* 2013
There Are Miracles in the Morning	*An Anthology of Northwest Poets,* 2013
Grace of Day	*Traveling in Company,* 2013
The Way It Was	*Traveling in Company,* 2013
Tears Like Rain	Alive Now Magazine, 2013
Behold the Stars	*Traveling in Company,* 2013
The Quiet of Snow	*Traveling in Company,* 2013
Baptized	*A Time for Singing* Magazine, 2012
Pearlescence	*Tidepools* Magazine, 2012
Night Rain	*Modern Liturgy,* 1989 *Lutheran Partners,* 1984

Other Books by the Author

The Mouse with Wheels in His Head
Fergus dreams of being the first mouse to ride the first Ferris Wheel at the 1893 World's Fair. But how is it to be done?

The Mouse Who Wanted to Fly
Fergus's second adventure takes him to Kitty Hawk where two brothers are going to fly the first airplane.
Should a mouse be on the first flight? Fergus thinks so.

Mischievous Max, A Teddy Bear Story
Max Bear is not a cuddly Teddy Bear. His eyes are beastly and his fur is scratchy. No wonder Leon doesn't want to sleep with him. What if Leon takes Max to bed for just one night? Does he know Max Bear likes to do mischief in the night?

Fergus of Lighthouse Island
This Fergus is named after a great uncle who loved adventure. You may have met him as he rode the first Ferris Wheel and flew with the Wright Brothers at Kitty Hawk. But this Fergus isn't brave at all. He's not looking for adventure. But when a hurricane threatens Lighthouse Island, adventure finds him.

Cloud Climber (An Adventure for Seven to Ten Year Olds)
When Seth and Emily spend a few weeks with their grandparents, they're sure it will be the most boring weeks of their lives. But there is no time to be bored after discovering Three Friends Hill, the Banshee's Cave, and a treasure found in the hayloft of the old barn.

All books available at Amazon.com
or the author's website: genegbradbury.com

GENE G. BRADBURY writes from his home in the Pacific Northwest where he lives with his wife, Debbie. His writing encompasses poetry, short stories, children's stories and education material for adults. He has self-published three children's books: *The Mouse with Wheels in His Head*, *The Mouse Who Wanted to Fly, Fergus of Lighthouse Island* and *Mischievous Max, A Teddy Bear Story.* His publications may be found in various children's magazines and adult periodicals. Gene teaches adult classes in theology in his area.

Gene has a B.A. in Philosophy, an M.Div. in Theology, and a Master's Degree in Spiritual Direction. Among his many interests he includes books and reading. He and Debbie collect books. A visit to their home is like a visit to a library. Gene is presently working on another children's picture book, a middle-grade chapter book, and a book of short stories. He is involved in numerous writers' workshops and enjoys sharing his stories during school visits.

BookWilde Children's Books

Visit the author's website:

genegbradbury.com

Made in the USA
San Bernardino, CA
13 March 2014